The "Write" Approach

BOOK I

Form Drawing for Better Handwriting

Joen Gladich
and
Paula A. Sassi

Rudolf Steiner College Press

ISBN 0-945803-19-2

INTRODUCTION

Teachers, businessmen and women all agree that handwriting has deteriorated. Much money and time are wasted due to illegible handwriting.

Why?

The formal way of teaching writing required too much time and repetition. So, there was a swing away from the formal teaching with nothing to replace it. The value of writing was denigrated, and in order to expedite the process machines (typewriters, computers) were introduced. This removed the necessity for the thorough teaching of handwriting.

Yet

Writing creates a basis on which students build skills for reading and communication. If Johnny writes, his reading improves.

Printing

Many students have reverted to printing, expressing a dislike of their writing because it looks ugly.

So

Book I is produced in order to help teachers, students, laymen to work towards **beautiful, clear handwriting** through form drawing. Book II will utilize these forms in the creation of letters that are pleasing to the eye.

> Your handwriting is you,
>
> Improve it!

CURSIVE WRITING

Free flowing comfortable writing is more "you" than printing can hope to be. Time spent in improving your handwriting is as meaningful as working creatively in any art form. The following exercises are aimed at developing SIMPLICITY, RHYTHM & BALANCE.

Also

The knowledge of how to form letters and how to connect them is paramount to clear legible writing.

DIRECTIONS

1. Walk the exercises, using available space.

2. Draw forms in the air with a large and free flowing movement. Follow the moving hand with the eyes.

3. If a chalkboard is available, draw the forms using standard chalk.

IF NOT AVAILABLE GO TO 4 & 5

4. Draw the forms with the finger on desk or table surface.

5. The student is now ready to draw the form on paper. After using the lined page, blank pages are provided for further practice of the forms. When the student feels that the form is drawn to the best of his ability - proceed to the next form. At each session do at least one line of the previously practiced forms.

ALL WRITING AND FORM DRAWING

IS MOVEMENT BROUGHT TO REST

Resist any temptation to bypass the need for large movements such as walking the forms or drawing them in the air. The value can only be appreciated through experience.

Watch your handwriting improve after you've moved!

POSITION IS EVERYTHING

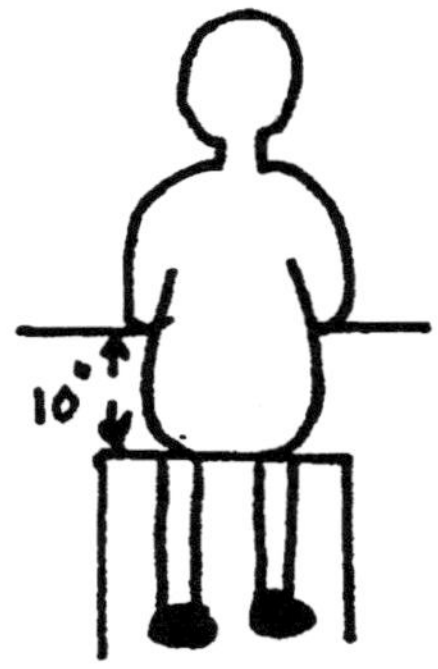

SEAT

1. Seating needs to be the correct height so feet rest flat on the floor.
2. Sit firmly on the seat with knees a little higher than hips.
3. The spine is slightly curved so that a crown could balance on the head.

DESK

1. Height of the desk should allow the writing arm to be close to the side of the body without pushing up the shoulder.
2. The forearm placement is such that the hand and arm up to approximately two inches below the elbow are on the writing surface.
3. The non-writing hand rests on the side of the paper, moving it up, so that the forearm remains in the correct position.

Attention to position promotes a feeling of well-being

PENCIL GRIP

The proper pencil grip is most important in the process of handwriting and may indicate learning handicaps when not done in the correct manner. The index finger and thumb of the writing hand should be used to hold the writing instrument. Only a mild amount of grip pressure is necessary in order to hold the instrument in place. The pen or pencil should then rest just below the first knuckle of the middle finger and be cradled between the thumb and index finger on the palm of the hand. The index finger should have a rounded arch to it and not a caved in appearance, white nails are in evidence when the pencil is held too tightly. The writing instrument should be held about one inch above the point. Writing employs the whole arm in movement and not just an up and down finger motion. Finger writing and tight pencil grip cause fatigue and tension.

LAZY EIGHT

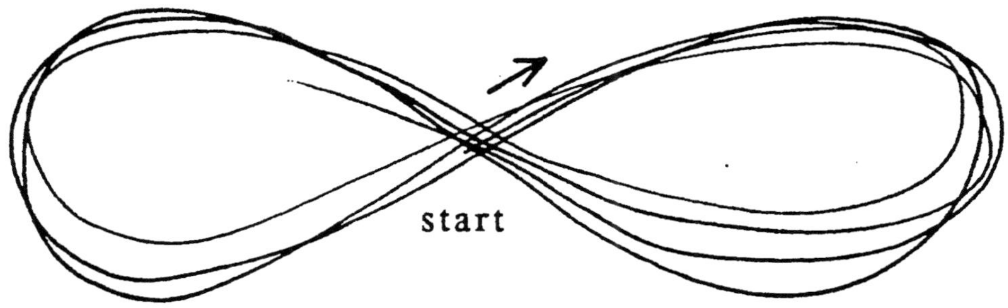

The Breather

The large movement of the lazy eight helps writing to be free flowing and relaxed. This exercise is recommended before each session and at approximately 15 minute intervals.

First, draw the lazy eight in the air with the right hand always being sure to move upward from the midline towards right and then left. Do this numerous times, then change to the left hand and do the same thing, both hands together to finish the exercise. Next, the teacher puts a large drawing on the board, large enough for students to need to stretch; not, however, outside of their reach. Students trace it continuously a number of times - do this exercise with left, right, then both hands together. It can next be done on their desk tops with the first finger, where the size will be somewhat constricted. Finally with a pencil on paper, using writing hand only.

Please pay attention that both movements from the midline are up and away - the crossing place is called the MIDLINE.

TWO WHEELS

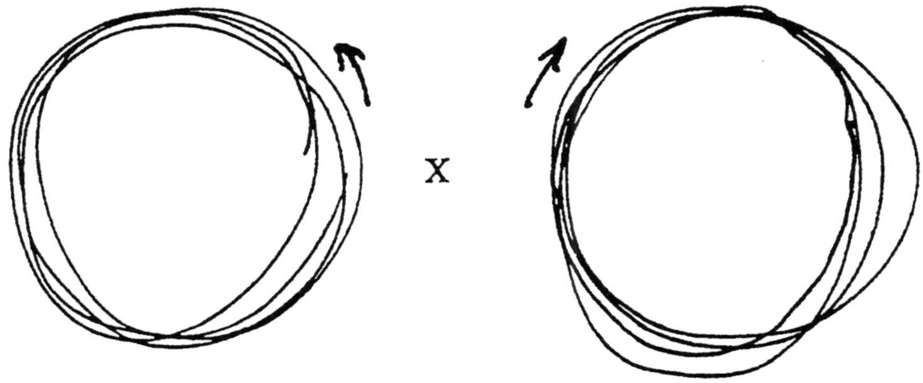

Left Right

The Balancer

The outward circular movement of the two wheels help achieve independent yet simultaneous movement of the two hands. This exercise is recommended before or after each session for stimulation.

This exercise is done on the board with chalk, using both hands and a piece of chalk in each. Place a cross on the board. The nose is brought close to the cross, almost touching it. Then, with a piece of chalk in each hand, begin to draw large circles in an up and away direction. The right hand will be circling in a clockwise direction, and the left, counter clockwise.

This exercise may prove difficult to some - all ages will benefit from it.

FORM

DRAWING

(Refer to directions on page iii)

I M P O R T A N T

A N N O U N C E M E N T

There are a number of blank pages in this book. These are located after each exercise and are to be used for practice. When these are filled and if you feel that there is still room for improvement, you may wish to procure more blank sheets of paper.

WE WISH TO TAKE THIS OPPORTUNITY TO WISH YOU ALL THE BEST RESULTS FROM YOUR WORK. MAY YOUR HAND-WRITING BECOME A JOY TO BEHOLD. THE PRACTICE OF THE FORMS WILL HELP YOU ATTAIN YOUR GOAL.

1. CUPS

a. Begin at the arrow.

b. Make half circles joined together in continuous, rhythmical movement.

c. Use the total line provided, then the partial lines and finally use the space with no lines, working from left to right, drawing forms as artistically as possible.

* Make sure that the forms are softly curved.

Always expect the very best of yourself!

2. HUMPS

a. Begin at the arrow.

b. Make half circles joined together in continuous, rhythmical movement.

c. Use the total line provided, then the partial lines and finally use the space with no lines, working from left to right, drawing forms as artistically as possible.

* Make sure that the forms are softly curved.

Are you doing your best?

3. PEAKS AND VALLEYS

a. Begin at arrow.

b. Make sharp angles, turn without lifting pencil or pen.

c. Carefully progress across to the right of the page.

d. Use the total line provided, then the partial lines and finally use the space with no lines, working from left to right, drawing forms as artistically as possible.

Are you working at your best level?

4. CUPS AND HUMPS

a. Begin with humps - do as in #2.

b. Place cups under humps, beginning about 1/2 way under the first hump, then continue with cups to the end of the line.

c. Use the total line provided, then the partial lines and finally use the space with no lines, working from left to right, drawing forms as artistically as possible.

Are you working carefully?

5. CUPS AND HUMPS INTERTWINED

a. Draw humps first - begin at the arrow.

b. Draw cups intertwined and reflecting humps.

c. Use the total line provided, then the partial lines and finally use the space with no lines, working from left to right, drawing forms as artistically as possible.

Taking care always pays off!

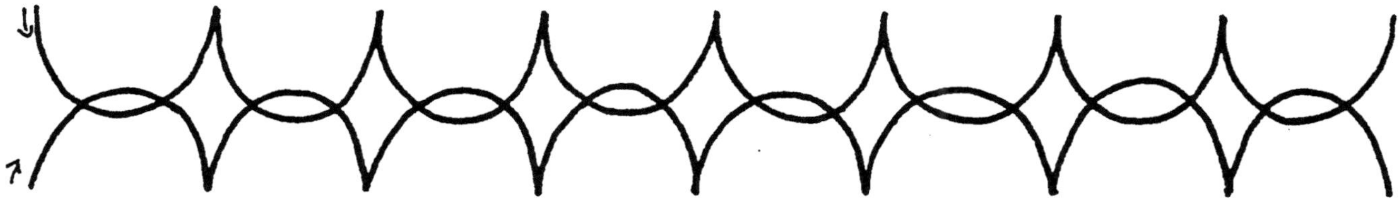

6. DIAMONDS

a. Draw one row of peaks and valleys on the line.

b. Draw a reflection directly under the first row.

c. Use the total line provided, then the partial lines and finally use the space with no lines, working from left to right, drawing forms as artistically as possible.

Have you made beautiful diamonds?

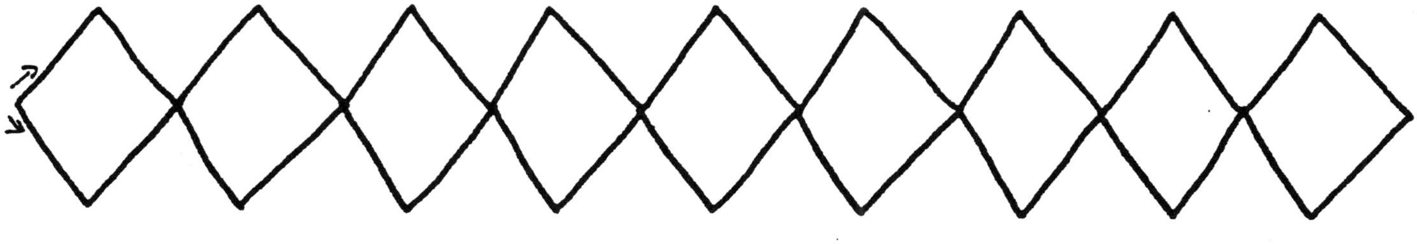

7. PEAKS AND VALLEYS INTERTWINED

a. Draw one row of peaks and valleys.

b. Begin at second arrow and intersect each down stroke and up stroke.

c. Use the total line provided, then the partial lines and finally use the space with no lines, working from left to right, drawing forms as artistically as possible.

You are doing your best work, aren't you?

8. LITTLE LOOPS

a. Draw these small loops all the way across the page. Be sure loops are open and can be seen through.

b. Use the total line provided, then the partial lines and finally use the space with no lines, working from left to right, drawing forms as artistically as possible.

Are your loops lovely curves and do they have a rhythm?

9. UPSIDE-DOWN LITTLE LOOPS

a. Draw small upside-down loops all the way across the page. Be sure loops show space through them.

b. Use the total line provided, then the partial lines and finally use the space with no lines, working from left to right, drawing forms as artistically as possible.

Was this harder than #8? You have done it well, haven't you?

10. LOOPS AND CUPS

a. Cups and loops drawn alternately across the page. You find a rhythm as you do them.

b. Use the total line provided, then the partial lines and finally use the space with no lines, working from left to right, drawing forms as artistically as possible.

You are surely doing your best, aren't you?

11. UPSIDE DOWN LOOPS AND CUPS

a. We now do the same as the previous form (#10), but draw them upside down, keeping the workbook in place.

b. Use the total line provided, then the partial lines and finally use the space with no lines, working from left to right, drawing forms as artistically as possible.

Is upside-down more difficult than right-side up?

12. REFLECTION

a. We are combining loops and cups and upside-down loops and cups (#10 and #11), first doing the upside-down loops and cups row (#11), then reflecting using loops and cups (#10). Be sure that loop reflects loop and cup reflects cup.

b. Use the total line provided, then the partial lines and finally use the space with no lines, working from left to right, drawing forms as artistically as possible.

This is quite a challenge, isn't it? Be sure to do your best!

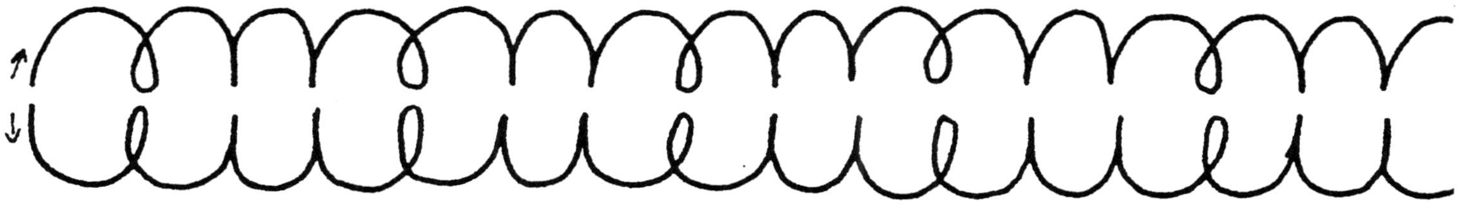

13. FLOWING WATER (RIPPLES)

a. Make these gentle curves really flow gently like water.

b. Use the total line provided, then the partial lines and finally use the space with no lines, working from left to right, drawing forms as artistically as possible.

This one was perhaps a little easier, but we must be sure to do our best!

14. OCEAN WAVES

a. These can be beautiful waves for surfing. Be sure you keep your pencil on the paper as you make this left/right curve. If you look carefully, you will see that the wave is about to crash. Can you see that?

b. Use the total line provided, then the partial lines and finally use the space with no lines, working from left to right, drawing forms as artistically as possible.

Did you do that beautifully?

15. DOUBLE WAVES

a. Draw one line of ocean waves as before (#14).

b. Now draw waves in between.

c. Use the total line provided, then the partial lines and finally use the space with no lines, working from left to right, drawing forms as artistically as possible.

That is a double whammy, but you did it well, didn't you?

16. CASTLE TOPS

a. Make nice round cups and join them together with a straight bar.

b. Use the total line provided, then the partial lines and finally use the space with no lines, working from left to right, drawing forms as artistically as possible.

Are you still expecting the best of yourself?

17. BIG AND LITTLE LOOPS

a. Be sure you can see through the big and little loops and don't squeeze them.

b. There to be a difference in height between little and big loops.

c. Use the total line provided, then the partial lines and finally use the space with no lines, working from left to right, drawing forms as artistically as possible.

You are doing your very best, I'm sure!

elle elle elle elle

18. BIG LOOP - CASTLE TOP

a. Big loop with a see-through space, castle top with a good straight line on top.

b. Use the total line provided, then the partial lines and finally use the space with no lines, working from left to right, drawing forms as artistically as possible.

Do you feel that you are doing well?

brbrbrbrbrbrbrbr

19. LOOP THE LOOP

a. All loops - top and bottom, to be seen through

b. Use the total line provided, then the partial lines and finally use the space with no lines, working from left to right, drawing forms as artistically as possible.

Isn't this great to do, but don't get carried away?

20. SWINGING BRIDGE

a. Draw tall, deep cups, which make the upright posts of the bridge (3 posts to a group.

b. Put the handrail across the posts 1/3 of the way from the top.

c. Use the total line provided, then the partial lines and finally use the space with no lines, working from left to right, drawing forms as artistically as possible.

Have you walked across a bridge like this? Is it sturdy?

21. UPSIDE DOWN LITTLE AND BIG LOOPS

a. Draw left to right small loops sitting on their heads on the line. (Groups of four)

b. Use the total line provided, then the partial lines and finally use the space with no lines, working from left to right, drawing forms as artistically as possible.

This was easy to do after all that practice! Yes? No?

22. LITTLE LOOP - PROPELLER

a. Little loop sits on the line, propellers long and straight in between. Be sure to keep the downstroke straight.

b. Use the total line provided, then the partial lines and finally use the space with no lines, working from left to right, drawing forms as artistically as possible.

Enjoy piloting across the page! Did you enjoy the flight?

efefefefefefefefefef

23. TEEPEES

a. Keep lines straight and make sharp angles with teepees resting on the line.

b. Use the total line provided, then the partial lines and finally use the space with no lines, working from left to right, drawing forms as artistically as possible.

Don't let it make you jumpy!

24. TEEPEES AND HUMPS FOR BALANCE

a. Do the top line first - angles and curves - keep one sharp and the other curved.

b. Reflect, as exactly as you can, what is on top.

c. Use the total line provided, then the partial lines and finally use the space with no lines, working from left to right, drawing forms as artistically as possible.

Your reflections are beautiful, I'm sure!

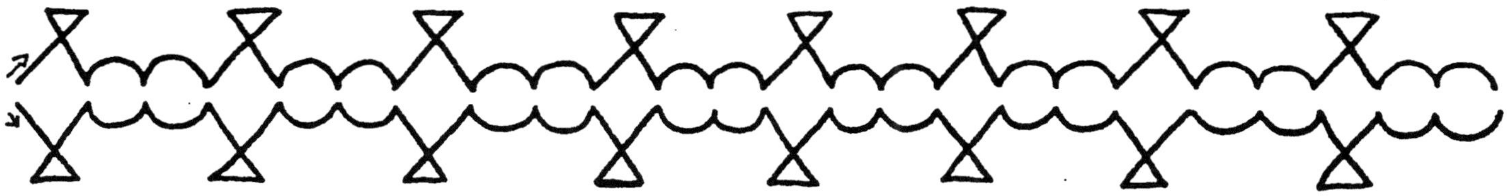

25. SPIRALS

a. Begin at the left and move inwards to the center. Start a new line and curve out and move to the next spiral. Keep these spirals as round as you can. Look at the example very carefully.

b. Use the total line provided, then the partial lines and finally use the space with no lines, working from left to right, drawing forms as artistically as possible.

Take on this challenge with a smile. You can do it!

ABOUT THE AUTHORS

JOEN GLADICH was born, raised and educated in England and taught in the city schools before marrying and coming to the United States after World War II. An active interest in her son's education kept her abreast of methods and changing styles and needs in schooling. During her son's college years she began to work with college students. This led to therapeutic work through handwriting analysis and graphotherapy, long time interests of Joen's. It became obvious that practical, corrective movement was needed to insure and anchor the developmental process. Joen continued to work and study in this field, became interested in Waldorf Education and took the teacher training in 1973.

These are some of the life experiences which led to the offering of the present manuals - THE WRITE APPROACH, Books I and II.

PAULA A. SASSI is a certified graphologist and consultant. She holds a B.A. degree in Psychology and a lifetime teaching credential in the California Community Colleges. She is president and owner of Handwriting Consultants International, a full time business offering graphological services and courses in handwriting analysis. Her work in Handwriting Movement Therapy with both children and adults prompted her to assist Joen in the writing of these books.

PRACTICE PAGE

DON'T STOP!

Get some unlined paper and keep practicing.